LOOK IT UP
Now in a fully revised edition

1 You and Your Body
2 People and Customs
3 What People Do
4 The Prehistoric World
5 Ships and Boats
6 People of Long Ago
7 The Sea
8 The Earth
9 Cold-Blooded Animals
10 Warm-Blooded Animals
11 Sport and Entertainment
12 The World of Machines
13 Land Travel
14 Flying
15 Outer Space
16 Index

Photo Credits: Heather Angel, M.Sc., F.R.P.S.; Australian News and Information Bureau; British Tourist Authority; Forestry Commission; Robert Harding Associates; Illustrated London News; Cees van der Meulen; New Civil Engineer; Pace Photography; John Parker; Picturepoint; Vidal Sassoon/Richard Lohr; Sutton Seeds; Toyota (U.K. Ltd.); United Kingdom Atomic Energy Authority; Thomas A. Wilkie Company; ZEFA.

Front cover: ZEFA.

Illustrators: Fred Anderson; Geoffrey Burns; Richard Eastland; Philip Emms; Dan Escott; John Fraser; Elizabeth Graham-Yool; Richard Hook; Eric Jewell; Ben Manchipp; Angus McBride; John Sibbick.

First edition © Macmillan Publishers Limited, 1979
Reprinted in 1981, 1982, 1983 and 1984
Second edition © Macmillan Publishers Limited, 1985

Chief Educational Adviser
Lynda Snowdon

Teacher Advisory Panel
Helen Craddock, John Enticknap, Arthur Razzell

Editorial Board
Jan Burgess, Rosemary Canter, Philip M. Clark, Beatrice Phillpotts, Sue Seddon, Philip Steele

Picture Researchers
Caroline Adams, Anne Marie Ehrlich, Gayle Hayter, Ethel Hurwicz, Pat Hodgson, Stella Martin, Frances Middlestorb

Designer
Keith Faulkner

Contributors and consultants
John E. Allen, Neil Ardley, Sue Becklake, Robert Burton, Barry Cox, Jacqueline Dineen, David J. Fletcher, Plantagenet Somerset Fry, Bill Gunston, Robin Kerrod, Mark Lambert, Anne Millard, Kaye Orten, Ian Ridpath, Peter Stephens, Nigel Swann, Aubrey Tulley, Tom Williamson, Thomas Wright

Published by Macmillan Children's Books
a division of Macmillan Publishers Limited
4 Little Essex Street, London WC2R 3LF
Associated companies throughout the world

ISBN 0 333 39721 5 (volume 3)
ISBN 0 333 39568 9 (complete set)

Printed in Hong Kong

What People Do

Second Edition

LOOK IT UP

Contents

	Page
WORKING IN SHOPS	4
The baker	6
The hairdresser	8
The shoemaker	9
The supermarket	10
WORKING ON THE LAND	12
Animal farming	14
Crop farming	16
Gardening	18
Working with trees	19
WORKING AT SEA	20
The fisherman	22
The merchant navy	24
Working on a lifeboat	26
Working on an oil rig	27
BUILDING AND CONSTRUCTION	28
The building site	30
Engineering	32

	Page
FACTORIES AND OFFICES	**34**
Working in a factory	**34**
The production line	**36**
Working with clothes	**38**
Working in an office	**40**
SERVICES	**42**
The policeman	**44**
The fireman	**46**
The postman	**48**
The dustman	**49**
The teacher	**50**
The librarian	**51**
Working in a hospital	**52**
The doctor	**54**
The nurse	**55**
The scientist	**56**
Working with money	**58**
Working on a newspaper	**60**
Working in a hotel	**62**
DID YOU KNOW?	**64**

WORKING IN SHOPS

The shops in this picture are in a place called a shopping 'precinct'. No cars are allowed on the street, so you do not have to worry about crossing the road. This makes shopping much easier. You can wander around, looking at the shops and deciding what to buy.

The baker sells bread and cakes. The butcher is standing outside his shop. He sells meat. Can you see the greengrocer? He sells fresh fruit and vegetables of all kinds.

The baker

You can buy fresh loaves of bread in the baker's shop. Sometimes the loaves are still warm from the oven when you buy them. Nowadays, most bread is made in factories and then taken to shops. Some bakers still bake their own bread. Then it is fresh, and good to eat.

First the baker mixes the dough. He uses flour and water and yeast. Yeast makes the bread 'rise'. If the baker did not put yeast into the dough, the loaves would be flat.

When the dough has been mixed, the baker takes it out of the bowl and kneads it. He turns the dough over and over, folding it and pushing it. This spreads the yeast out well.

The baker shapes the loaves before baking them. He makes both big and small loaves. Many bakers also make round loaves and cottage loaves.

The baker leaves the loaves to 'rise'.
When they are the right size, the
baker puts them in the oven.
He leaves them there until they are
brown and crusty on top.

The bread is ready. The baker takes
it out of the oven and leaves it to
cool for a while. Then he takes the
bread into the shop. It is still warm
and smells delicious.

In the shop, customers can choose
from many different kinds of bread.
They can buy white or brown bread.
They can also buy loaves in different
shapes. Some bakers also sell
croissants, pastries and cakes.

The hairdresser

Hairdressers work in shops called salons. Customers go to a salon to have their have cut, or washed and set. Sometimes they ask the hairdresser to give them a new hair style. Some salons have departments for men and women. Shops which are just for men's hairdressing are called barbers' shops.

The hairdresser is shampooing a customer's hair. She washes it with shampoo and then rinses it.

Hairdressers usually cut hair when it is wet.

Hairdressers sometimes use a conditioner to keep the hair healthy. They can also use dyes to make people's hair a different colour.

Some customers like their hair curled. The hairdresser winds the hair around rollers while it is wet.

Sometimes people dye their hair a different colour by themselves. In Kenya and Tanzania Masai warriors dye their hair with red clay.

The hairdresser dries the customer's hair with a hair dryer. This takes quite a long time.

The shoemaker

Very few shoemakers still make shoes. Today, most shoes are made in factories. Shoemakers mend shoes. They put on new soles and heels when they wear out. Soles and heels are often made of leather.

This shoemaker is fixing on a heel. He is making sure that the sole is fixed to the rest of the shoe.

Heel bars are places where shoes are mended quickly. People wait while the repairs are done.

The supermarket

In many shops, you buy the goods from the shopkeeper or from assistants. In supermarkets, you serve yourself, and pay for all the goods at the check-out as you leave. In large supermarkets you can buy all sorts of goods, from fruit and vegetables to clothes and electrical goods.

car park

check-out

enquiries

automatic doors

restaurant

main entrance

trolleys

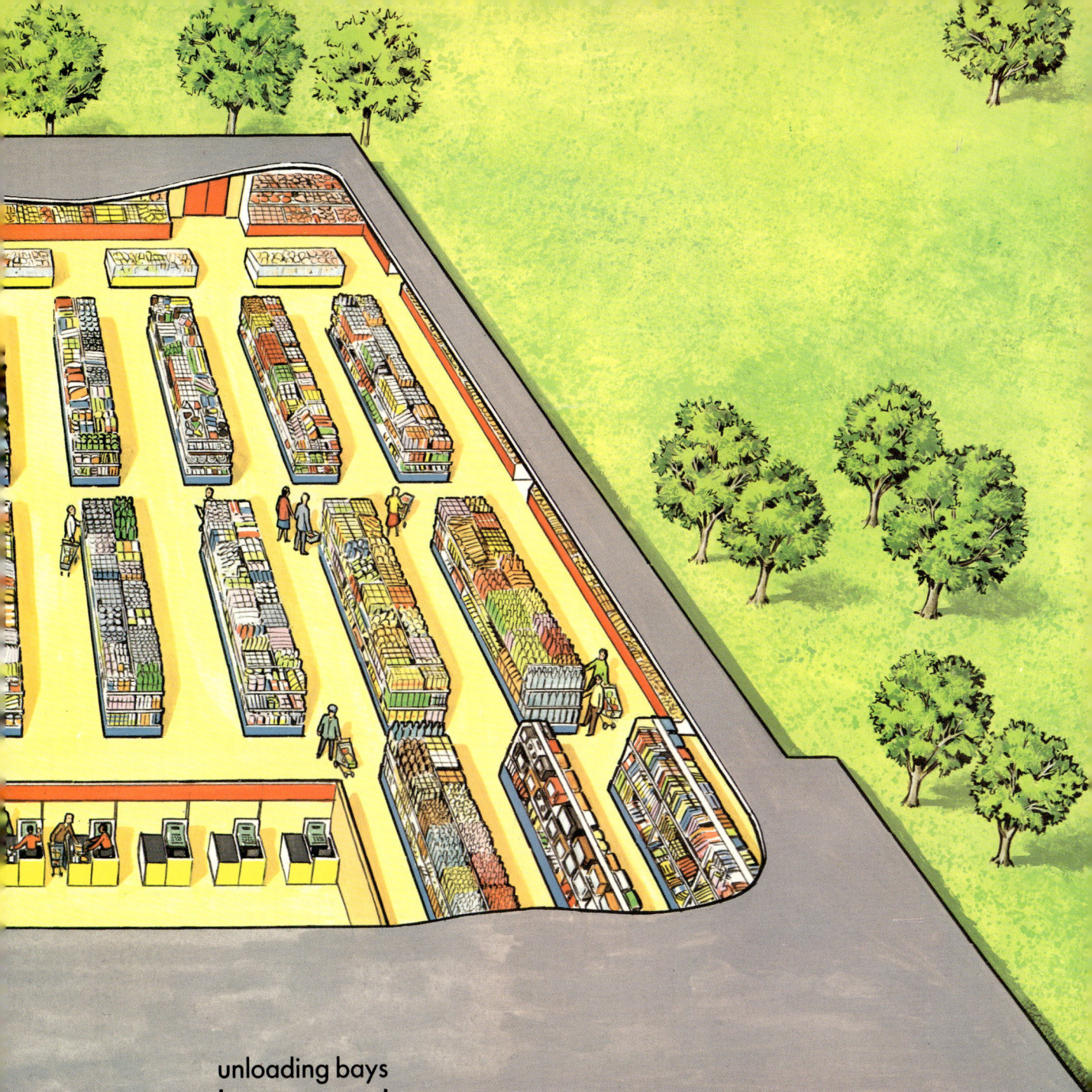

unloading bays

refuse disposal

delivery area

11

WORKING ON THE LAND

Farmers supply most of the food that
we eat. Some farmers keep animals
such as sheep and cattle to provide
milk and meat. Other farmers grow
fruit, vegetables and crops such as
wheat, barley and rye.

silo

potato harvesting

dairyman

dairy

farm manager

sheepshearing

fruitpicking

vet

fence
repairers

blacksmith

cropspraying

Lots of people work on this large farm. They pick the fruit and vegetables, milk the cows, shear the sheep and harvest the corn. Farmers have to work very hard.

office

farmhouse

haymaking

collecting milk

Animal farming

Certain animals are very important to us. They provide us with things we need to live. Animals like this are called 'domesticated' because they are no longer wild. We get milk from cows and wool from sheep.

In Australia many cattle stations are so big that the cattle have to be rounded up by men on horses. Sometimes the cattle are taken many miles to find good grazing land. These farms are called ranches.

ostrich

reindeer

llama

Oysters are a kind of shellfish.
Many people like to eat them.
On this oyster farm the oysters are
being collected from the 'beds'.

In other parts of the world different
animals are domesticated. In Lapland
it is very cold. People who live there
keep reindeer to pull sledges and to
give them milk. In the desert it is very
hot. Camels can store water so they
are used for travel. In South America
llamas are kept to provide wool and
meat. Llama wool is very silky. Some
people breed pheasants for their meat.

pheasant

In the winter sheep grow thick
woolly coats to keep them warm.
They have to be dipped in a special
liquid. This liquid keeps their coats
clean and keeps their skins healthy.

15

Crop farming

Farmers grow grain crops such as barley and wheat. First the farmer ploughs the field. He turns the soil over, as if he were digging the garden. This breaks up the soil.

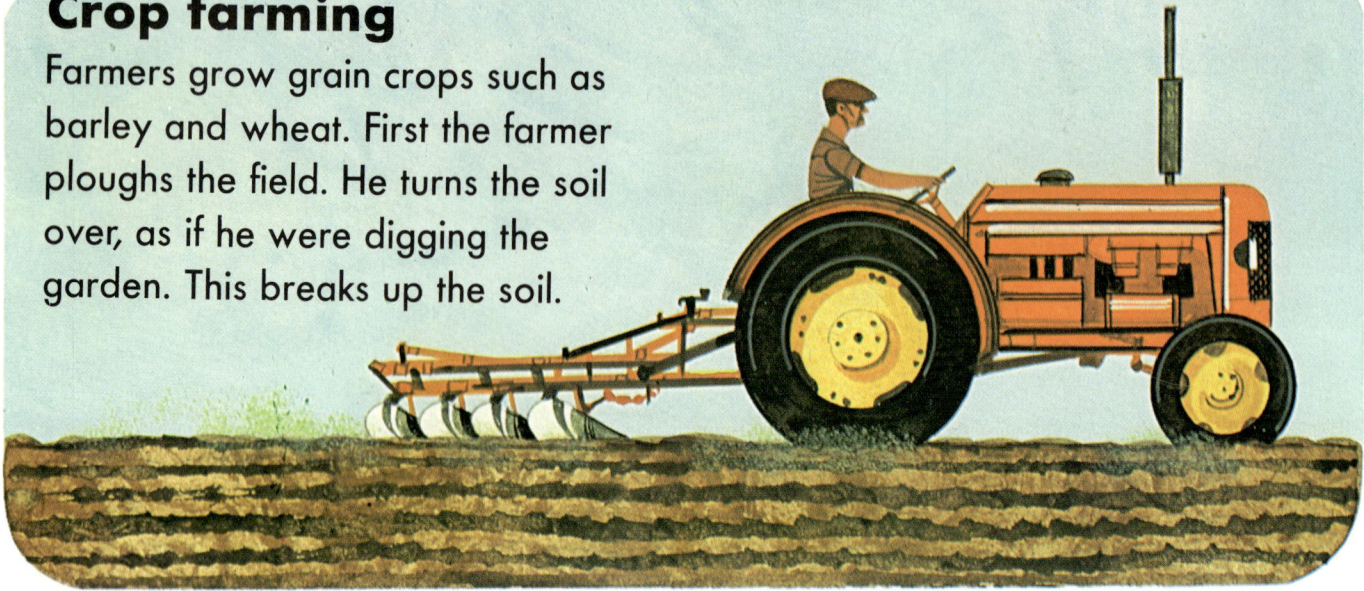

Next, the seeds are sown. This is often done by a machine. The machine sprinkles the seeds in rows. Not all the seeds will grow.

Some of the seeds will be eaten by birds and some will die, so the farmer plants more than he will need. When the seeds begin to grow, small green plants appear. They need plenty of sun and rain to grow into strong, healthy plants. Barley and wheat turn yellow when they are ripe.

When the crops are ready they are picked. This is called 'harvesting'. Barley, wheat and other cereal crops are gathered with a combine harvester. This cuts down the plants. Then it separates the grain or 'ears' from the stalks. The stalks are made into straw bales. Grain is put in sacks.

Some straw is kept for animals to sleep on in the winter. The grain is sent to the mills. In the mills it is made into flour for bread and cakes.

Gardening

Many people enjoy gardening. They do it when they are not working. They grow vegetables and flowers for their families. Some people look after gardens as a job. Big gardens need several gardeners. They keep the flower beds and vegetable garden tidy. They also put in new plants all the year round: Many gardeners also work in parks.

Nurseries are places where plants and flowers are grown. Many plants are grown in greenhouses so that they will not die in the winter. People go to nurseries to buy plants to put in their own gardens. Florists buy cut flowers. Holland is famous for its fields of tulips.

Working with trees

Trees are specially planted in places called tree plantations. Foresters plant the trees and look after them. Sometimes trees have to be cut down for timber. This is called felling. Foresters cut down the trees with big chain saws. The wood is used to make furniture and other goods.

WORKING AT SEA

Many people work at sea. There are
jobs to be done on different kinds of
boats. The big ship is a passenger
ferry, which takes people from one
place to another. Fishermen go out in
trawlers to catch fish. Submarines
can dive beneath the waves and
travel underwater. In some jobs
people stay at sea for a long time.

passenger ferry

trawler

submarine

People work at sea in other ways too. They build rigs to drill for oil from the ocean bed. Astronauts sometimes land on the sea. They are let out of their space capsule by frogmen. Lighthouses warn of the danger of rocks. If a boat sinks, its crew can be rescued by lifeboat or helicopter.

helicopter

oil rig

lighthouse

space capsule

lifeboat

70-001

The fisherman

Most of the fish we eat comes from the sea. Fishermen go out to sea in boats to catch them. Sometimes boats stay at sea for several days. The big picture on the right shows fishermen in the Seychelles. They are fishing with a seine net. This is a big net with floats around the top. This net can be used from the shore.

Fishermen unload their fish at seaside towns. These towns are called fishing ports. They are usually in sheltered bays with a harbour. Boats are moored in the harbour at night, or when the weather is bad.

The captain of a large fishing boat has to navigate the boat to the fishing grounds. He finds a good place to fish by looking for green water. Fish eat tiny animals called plankton. These animals make the water green. When the captain sees the green water, he knows it is a good place to fish.

When the captain has found a good place to fish, the crew get the nets ready. The nets spread out from the boat. Sometimes nets go right down to the bottom of the sea. The crew wait till the nets are full.

Have you ever eaten fresh fish? In some seaside towns fishermen catch fish and sell it the same day. People buy the fish and cook it. It tastes delicious.

The Merchant Navy

People in the Merchant Navy work on ships that carry cargo or passengers. This ship is carrying cargo to another country. The cargo is stored in the middle and the front of the ship. Some of the crew are tying the cargo to the deck to keep it secure. Other members of the crew are working in the engine room, eating or sleeping.

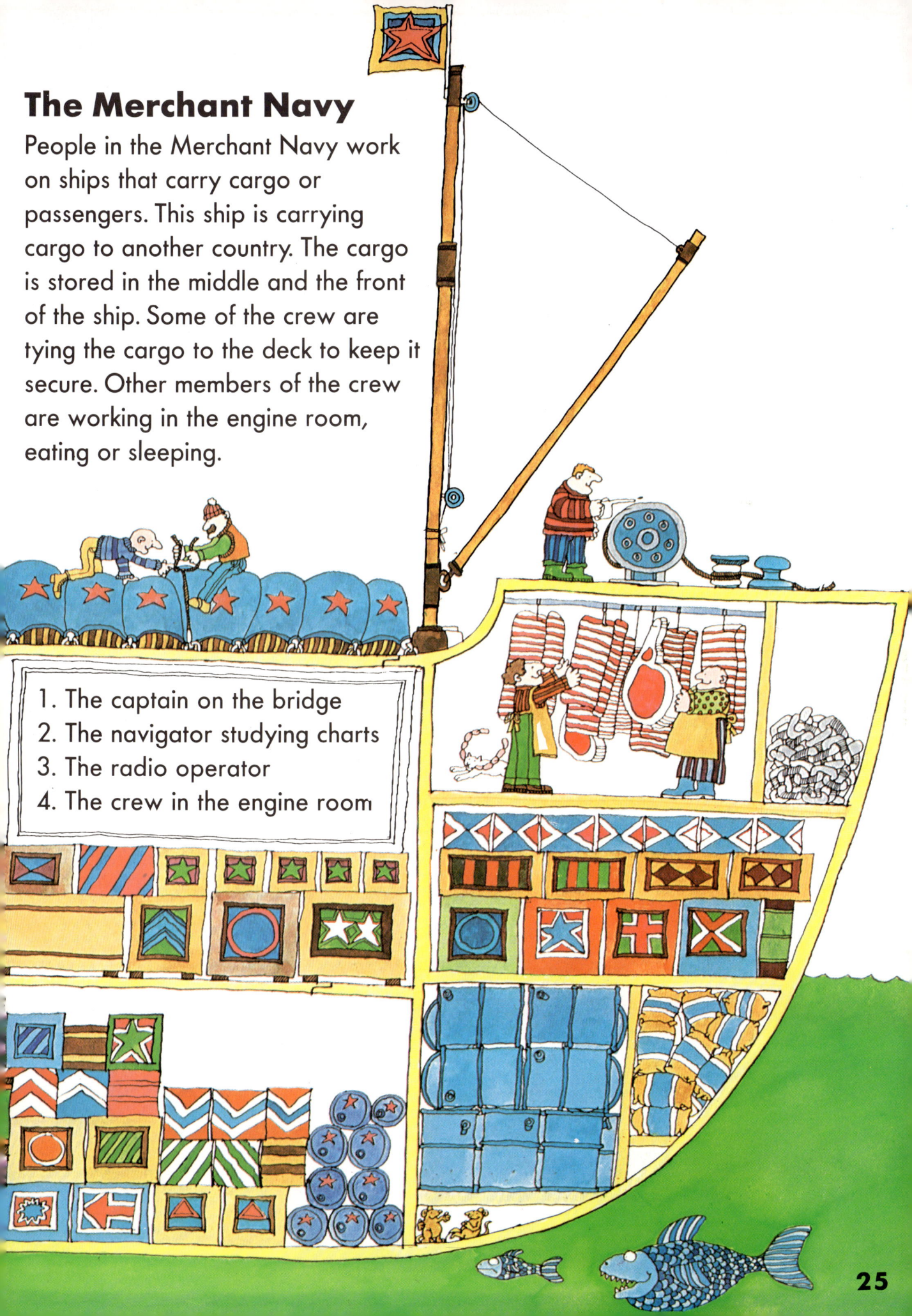

1. The captain on the bridge
2. The navigator studying charts
3. The radio operator
4. The crew in the engine room

Working on a lifeboat

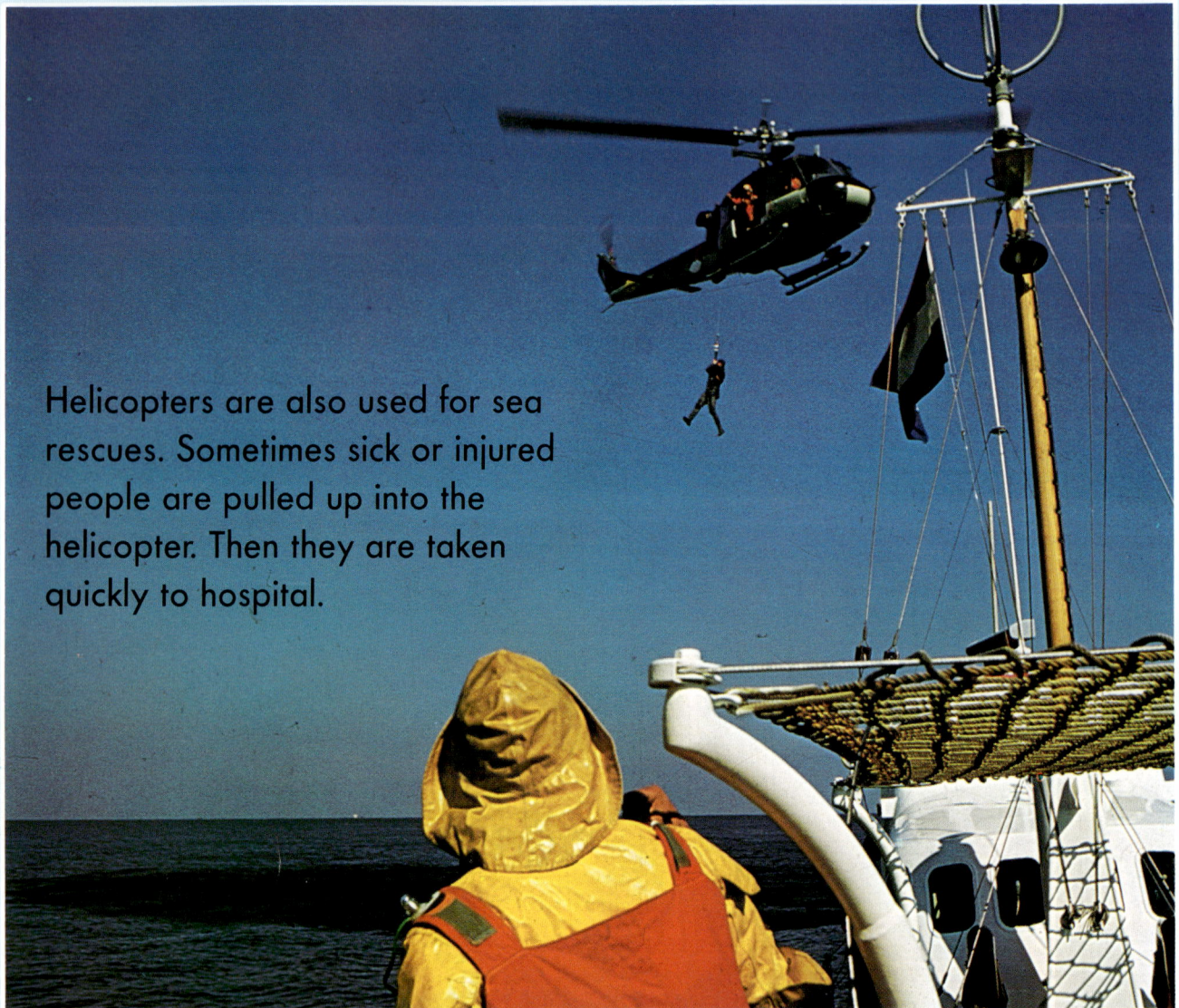

Helicopters are also used for sea rescues. Sometimes sick or injured people are pulled up into the helicopter. Then they are taken quickly to hospital.

Most seaside towns have a lifeboat. Lifeboatmen are usually volunteers. This means that they have another job as well. They have to be ready to leave their job and go out to sea when a ship is in danger. The sea is very rough when they go out.

derrick man

Working on an oil rig

The drilling superintendent is in charge of an oil rig. The drilling engineer controls the instruments. The derrick man works on the platform. Roustabouts do jobs such as changing bits of the drill. Many jobs on oil rigs need a lot of skill.

A-22

crane

roustabout

radio room

canteen

divers' room

drilling engineer

science laboratory

drilling superintendent

27

BUILDING AND CONSTRUCTION

A lot of people are needed to build a house. They all have different skills. First, someone chooses the land where the house will be built. Then an architect designs the house. Someone else orders materials to build with, like bricks and wood.

A house needs walls and floors, a roof, water and light, doors and windows. No single person knows how to do the work to complete all these things. Each job needs a different person to do it.

A quantity surveyor makes sure that the house is built properly. He finds people to do the different jobs and works out the cost of the materials.

The 'foundations' of the house are underground. Men dig trenches and then fill them in with concrete to support the house.

A bricklayer builds the brick walls. He stands on 'scaffolding' to build the high parts. Carpenters put in the wooden parts such as floor boards.

The architect works closely with the surveyor. She designs the house and prepares drawings which show both the inside and the outside.

Before work can begin, the ground has to be cleared. A bulldozer is used to flatten the land. The driver makes sure the land is flat.

The plumber lays pipes so that the house has a supply of water. The electrician makes sure that the lights and heating work properly.

Last of all, the house is painted by decorators. They paint the walls and woodwork to protect them and make them look nice.

The building site

bricklayer

carpenter

plumber

tiler

Here you can see all the people working on a house. Look at the cement mixer. When the cement is ready the bricklayer uses it to stick the bricks together. One man is carrying the bricks to the bricklayer. He carries them in a 'hod'. The men putting tiles on the roof are called tilers. Plumbers are fitting the radiators inside the house.

bulldozer

electrician

cement mixer

decorator

quantity surveyor

31

Engineering

Engineers work out the best way to make things. Some engineers make things that move, like aeroplanes, ships, cars, railway engines and rockets for going into space. Some engineers find ways of improving machines. They work out how to save fuel and how to make machines work faster.

Some engineers work on buildings. They are called civil engineers. They make sure that the right machines and materials are used, so that the building will not fall down. The engineer in the picture above is working on an enormous block of offices. He is studying the plans of the building.

In the big picture you can see some of the things that engineers do. They build bridges and roads as well as buildings and factories. Have you seen one of the huge suspension bridges that span wide rivers and estuaries? Engineers plan them so that they are safe for traffic. They also design machines.

This engineer is using a 'walkie talkie'. This is a small radio used to talk to people near by. The engineer is working on a building. He has to talk to men who are high up on the scaffolding, to tell them what to do. His hard hat protects him.

nurse

canteen

office manager

designing

foreman

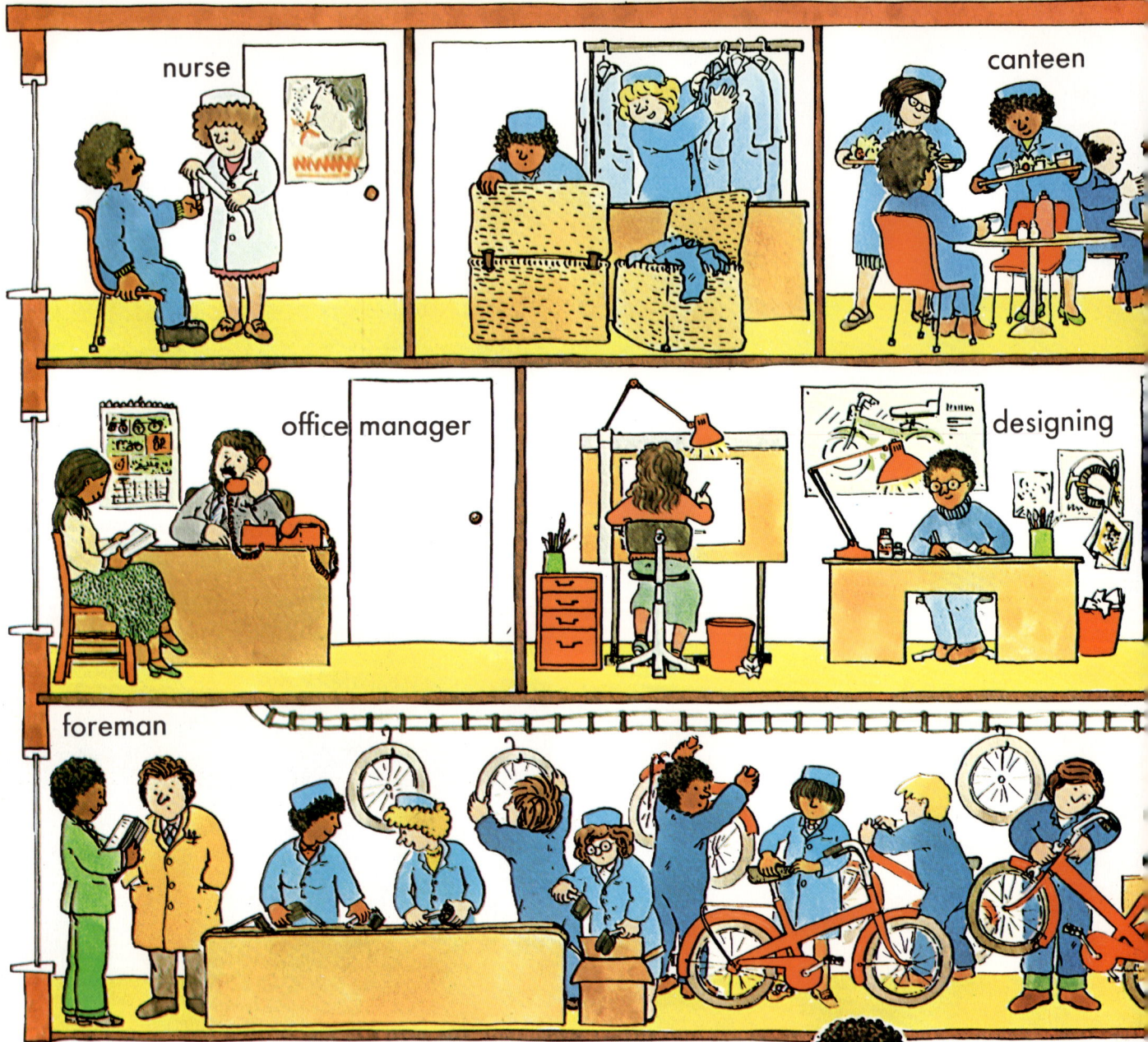

FACTORIES AND OFFICES

Working in a factory

Most of the things we use everyday are made in factories. The factories are specially organized so that a lot of the same sort of things can be made very quickly. This factory makes bicycles.

testing

welding

production line

store

People in factories see the nurse if they are ill. They eat in the canteen. In the design studio new kinds of bicycles are planned. A sample bicycle is made and tested to make sure there is nothing wrong with the design. Different parts of the bicycle are made in the welding room.

The production line

Machines are often put together on production lines. Cars are normally built in this way. They are not built one by one, but passed along a line so that the various parts of the car can be fitted together. Each job, such as welding, screwing and drilling, must be done hundreds of times each day. Some jobs are done by people. Others are done by automatic machines or 'robots'.

The car soon takes shape on the
production line. One of the most
important jobs to be done is the
painting. Paint protects the metal
from rust.

The man working in this factory in Germany is using a machine to make embroidered ribbon. The ribbons will be used to decorate clothes.

Working with clothes

Clothes are made from many different types of material. Cotton is made from cotton plants. Wool comes from sheep. Other materials, such as nylon, are made by men. The nylon is made in factories. In the picture below a Thai woman is preparing silk.

Designers draw patterns for the clothes. The material is then cut out. The pieces are sewn together with sewing machines. These women are making dresses in a factory in Brazil.

Clothes are sold in shops and also in boutiques. Shop assistants help customers to find clothes that are the right size and that look nice.

Working in an office

This is an open-plan office. All the people work in a big open space. The boss, however, has her own office. The receptionist sits at the entrance to the office. When visitors come she shows them where to go. Two visitors are waiting for the boss.

telephonist

Secretaries type letters, answer the
phone and file away letters.
The telephonist answers the phone.
She switches the calls through to the
right people by using the switchboard.

boss

receptionist

secretary

Start here

1

2

3

4 5 6 7

Bottom falls out of dustbin Go back 1

SERVICES

We often meet the people you can see in this game. They all do jobs that help us in some way. You may see some of them on your way to school. Perhaps you will see a postman, or a policeman on road duty.

Collect pencil case from Lost Property Move on 3

Knock over librarian's books Go back 6

47 46 45 44 43 42 41 40 39 3

48

49

Doctor mends arm Move on 3

Hurt your arm Back 1

Taxi driver takes you home to finish

50 51 52 53 54 55 56 57 58

Drop pencil case
Back 1

14

13

Dog chases postman
away Back 3

12 Policeman sees you
across road to 24

24

15 **16** **17** **18** **19** **20** **21**

22

23

25

Roadsweeper finds
pencil case
Move on 3

26

27

9 **10** **11**

Correct sum for
teacher
extra throw

7+2

28

Busdriver won't wait
Miss 1 throw

37 **36** **35** **34** **33** **32** **31** **30** **29**

Home for tea

When you get to school, you will
see your teacher. Perhaps the
librarian will lend you a book from
the school library. If you are ill, you
may have to go to the doctor.
These people do not make or sell
things, but they all do jobs that are
very necessary to our lives.

60 **61** **62** Finish

Dutch policeman

English policewoman

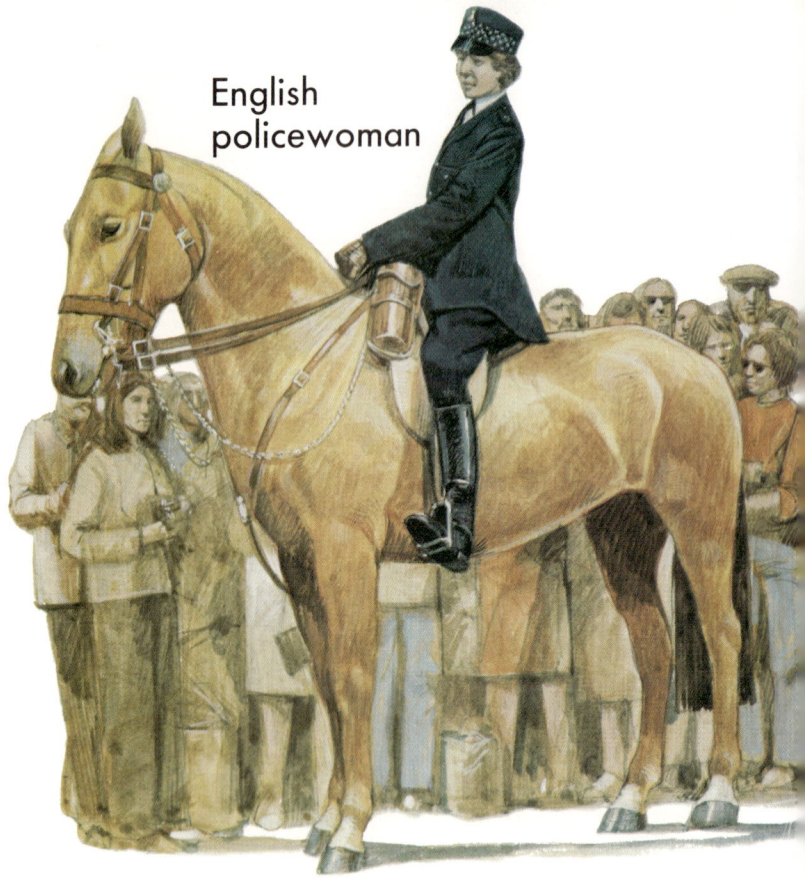

French policeman

The policeman

If you are ever lost, ask a policeman to show you the way. Policemen patrol everywhere. Some walk about the streets. Others go in cars, on motor cycles, or in police boats. When there are large crowds, policemen also patrol on horseback. They keep the crowds in order.

Policemen catch people who are doing something wrong, like stealing. They also find out what happened at motor accidents.

This policeman is directing traffic in India. It is very hot there, so he has an umbrella to shade him from the sun. He is standing on a platform so that people in cars can see him more easily as they drive along.

In the summer many people go away by car. Sometimes there are traffic jams. Policemen fly over the roads in helicopters to see the traffic. They tell people the roads are busy.

Policemen make sure that people are not going too fast on the roads. Their own cars go very fast to overtake people who are speeding.

The fireman

Firemen work from a fire station.
This is where the fire engine is kept.
Firemen are always ready for an
emergency. They can get to a fire
very quickly. Sometimes they use
special foam to put out a fire.
You can see this in the picture below.

Firemen do other jobs too.
They rescue people who are stuck in
lifts. Sometimes cats won't come
down from trees. Firemen bring them
down. Can you see the boy in the
well? The firemen will rescue him.

Firemen have to train a lot before they are ready to go to fires. There are big ladders on fire engines. Firemen practise using the ladders, so that they can rescue people trapped on high buildings.
Firemen do not only put out fires. They help during floods, too.

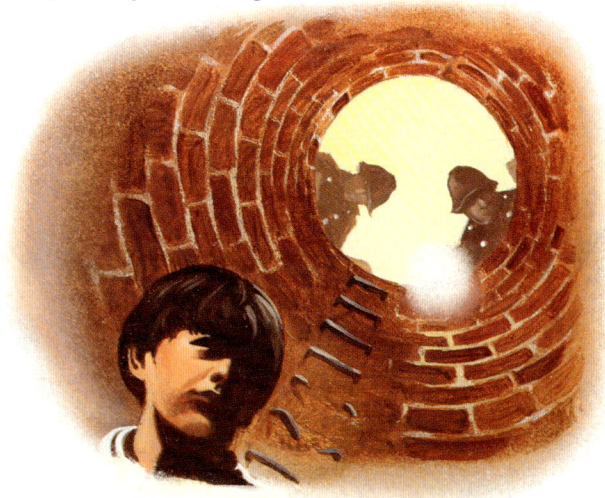

The postman

The postman's job is to see that letters and parcels go to the right places. Some postmen collect letters. Other postmen deliver letters. What happens when you post a letter in a pillarbox or when you take a parcel to the post office?

1

First, the postman collects all the letters and parcels. He takes them to the sorting office.

2

The letters have to be sorted, so that they go to the right places. Machines can help to do this.

3

Mail goes by train to the towns. Then it is taken to the post office.

4

In the post office the letters are sorted. Here, people are sorting the letters into boxes. Then the letters are put in sacks.

5

The postman collects the letters from the post office. He brings the mail to your house.

The dustman

The dustman takes away rubbish from the streets and from our homes. He goes to all the houses and collects the dustbins. Then he empties the rubbish into a lorry.

The lorry takes the rubbish to a place called a 'tip'. These tips are usually out of the centre of towns. Sometimes the rubbish is burnt. Dustmen often work early in the morning, before many people are up.

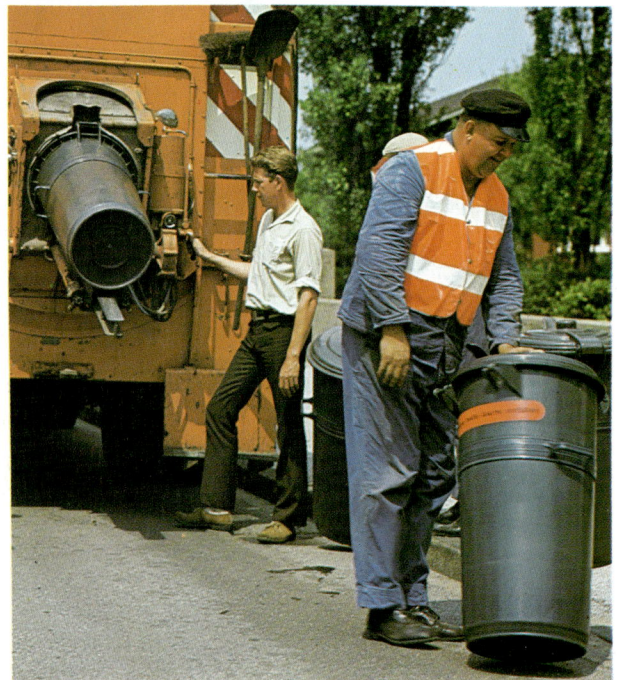

The teacher

Teachers in primary schools teach all subjects. In secondary schools, teachers usually teach only one subject. They have to know all about their subject and help their children to understand what they learn.

The class in the picture on the right is in Sri Lanka. The weather in Sri Lanka is hot, so the teacher can teach some lessons outside.

Some teachers teach subjects like games, music and dancing. This dancing lesson is taking place in a school in North Africa.

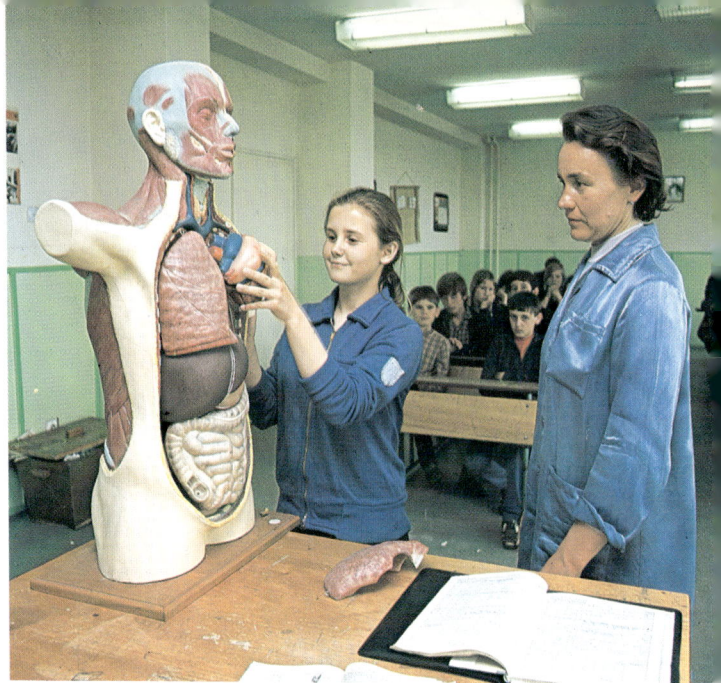

Teachers usually work in a classroom. This lesson is about how the body works. The teacher is using a model to show the different parts of the body. The children have to learn the names of the different parts and where they are found.

The librarian

A library is a place where people can go to borrow books. They can study in the library, too. So they can use lots of different books without having to take them home. Many schools have libraries.

A librarian is someone who looks after a library. Librarians keep a record of everyone who borrows books. They know a lot about the books and can give people advice and answer their questions.

Working in a hospital

When you are ill you sometimes have to go to hospital. The people who work in hospitals have learnt all about illness. They know how to help sick people get better. Doctors and nurses work in hospitals. There are other people working there too.

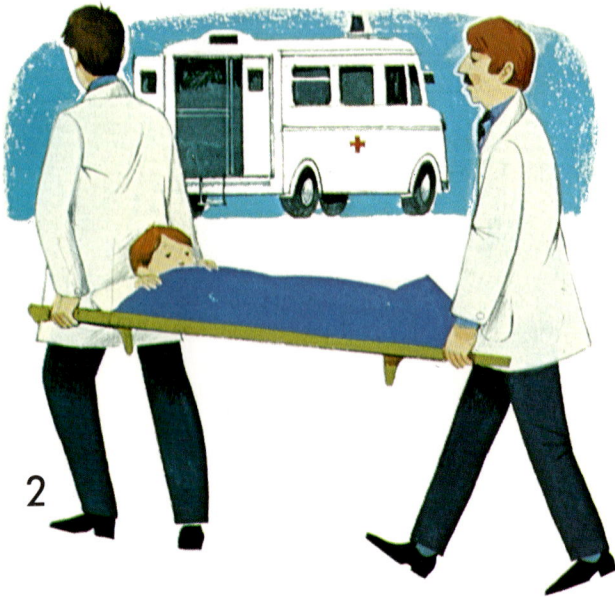

1

This boy has fallen and hurt his leg.
A man is giving him first aid.
He keeps the boy still, so that he will not hurt himself any more.

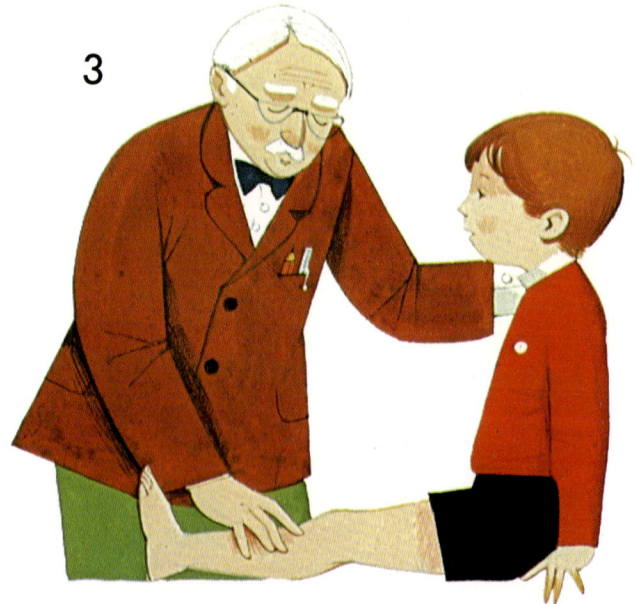

2

Then the ambulance arrives.
The ambulance men put the boy on a stretcher. Then they drive him to the nearest hospital.

3

The doctor at the hospital goes to see the boy. He examines the boy's leg and finds that it is broken.

4

The boy cannot walk because his leg hurts. The porter comes along with a wheelchair. He wheels the boy to the ward.

5

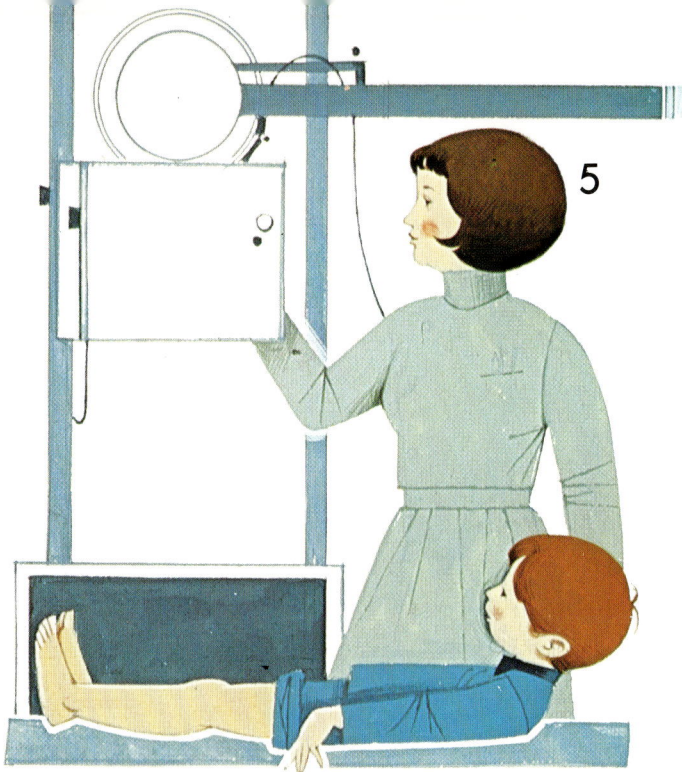

The radiographer x-rays the boy's leg to find out how the bone is broken. An x-ray is a picture of the inside of the body. It shows the bones and the parts between them.

6

The doctor decides to put the leg in plaster. This will keep the leg straight, so the bone can set.

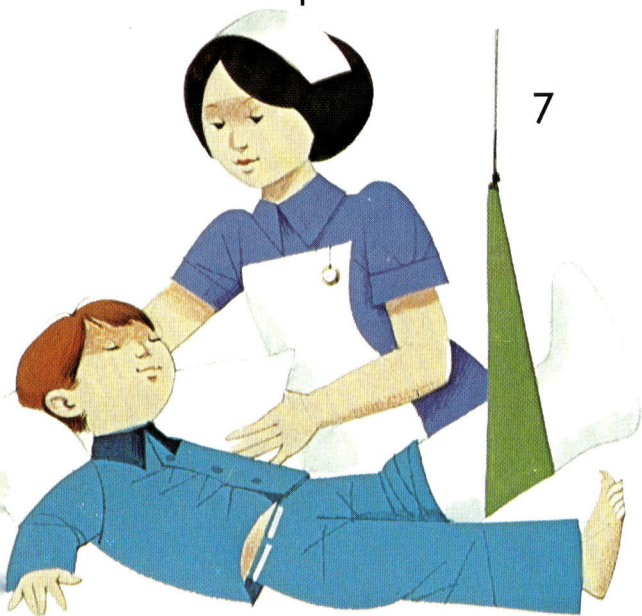

7

While the boy is in the ward he is looked after by a nurse. She makes sure that he is comfortable. She will bring him meals, too.

After a few days the boy gets out of bed. His leg is stiff from being in plaster. A physiotherapist help him to exercise it.

8

The doctor

In parts of Australia the towns are far apart. The doctor may live a long way away. He goes by plane to see his patients, so he is called the 'flying doctor'.

Not all doctors work in hospitals. Many doctors see their patients in the 'surgery'. A surgery is a place where people can go if they are ill but do not need to go to hospital.

The doctor sees her patients and finds out what is wrong with them. Then she tells them what kind of medicine will make them better. Sometimes doctors give injections. An injection stops you from catching a disease.

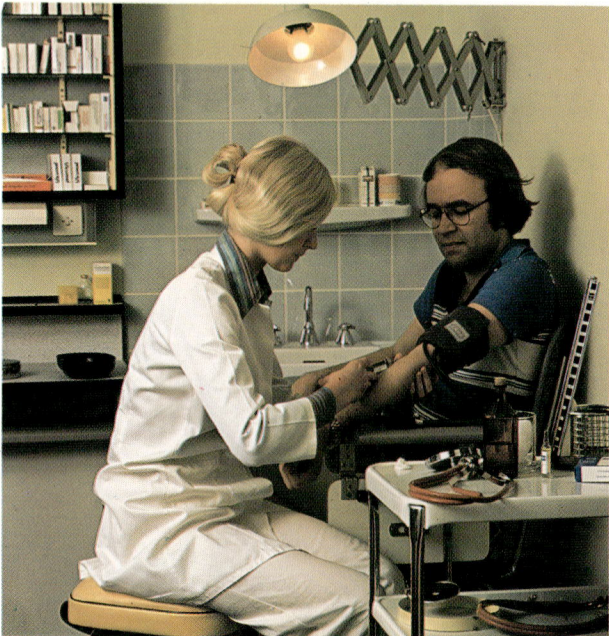

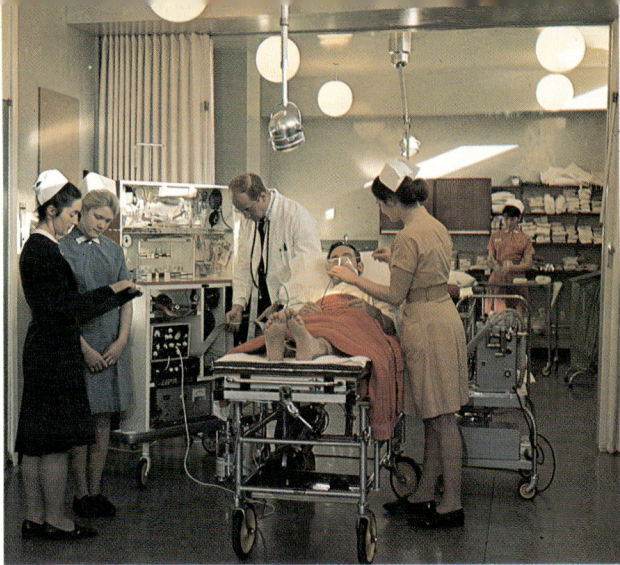

The nurse

Nurses usually work in hospitals. They look after people who are ill in bed. Nurses give their patients medicine and make them comfortable. If a patient cannot breathe properly, a nurse will give him oxygen to help him get better.

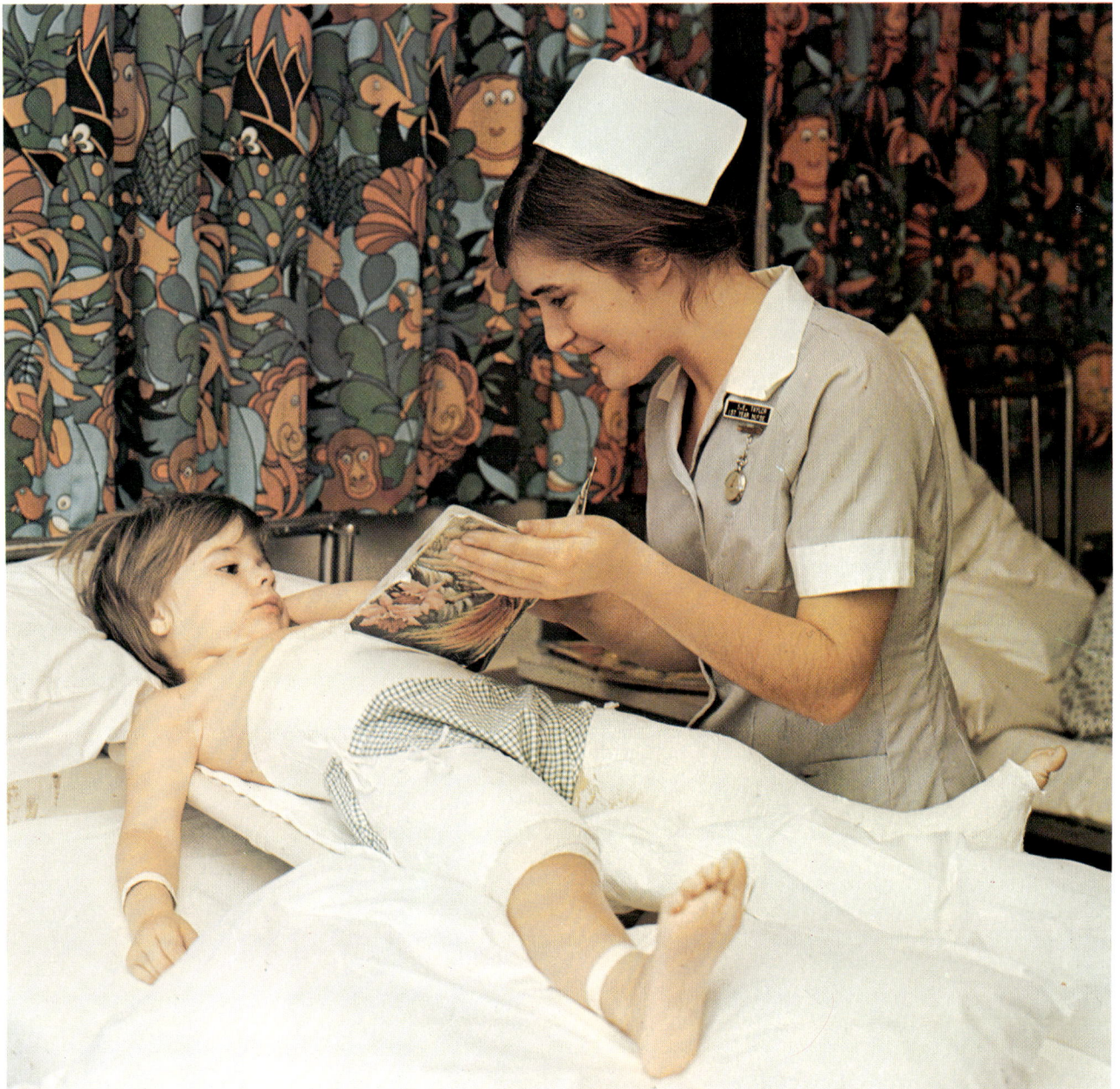

The scientist

All scientists try and discover more about the way things work and why things happen. Some scientists do experiments to find new medicines and new types of food. Other scientists study the past. They try to find out how life began. Some scientists study how people lived a long time ago.

Scientists need to find out whether new medicines will work. They use animals to help them with their experiments. In the picture on the left, a snake is being used.

Archaeologists find remains of old buildings. They study them to see how people lived a long time ago.

This scientist is in her laboratory. She is experimenting with chemicals in test tubes. She is studying what happens to the chemicals.

Scientists study the weather too. They use instruments to measure rainfall, sunshine, wind and clouds.

Working with money

Everyone needs money. Without money you cannot buy the things you need to live, such as food and clothes. Money can be banknotes or coins. It is made in a place called the mint. The mint produces all the money that is made in a country. No one else can make coins.

New money is taken to banks to be kept safely. Security men take it there so that it will not be stolen on the way. They travel in special vans.

Many people keep the money that they earn in a bank. The bank keeps their money safe until they want it. Then they go and cash a cheque from the cashier. They can cash just the amount of money they need to buy things.

Customers pay the shopkeeper when they buy things in his shop. The shopkeeper puts all the money that he takes into a till.

At the end of the day, the shopkeeper counts up all the money in the till. Then he takes it along to the bank. He does this every day. Most businesses keep their money in banks, not in their offices.

The shopkeeper pays in the money to the cashier. The cashier counts it all out and writes down the amount.

Working on a newspaper

Working on a newspaper is a very busy job. Many newspapers are printed each day, and they have to have all the latest news in them. The editor is in charge of the paper. Reporters find out the news stories and write them. The paper is printed so that it is on sale every morning.

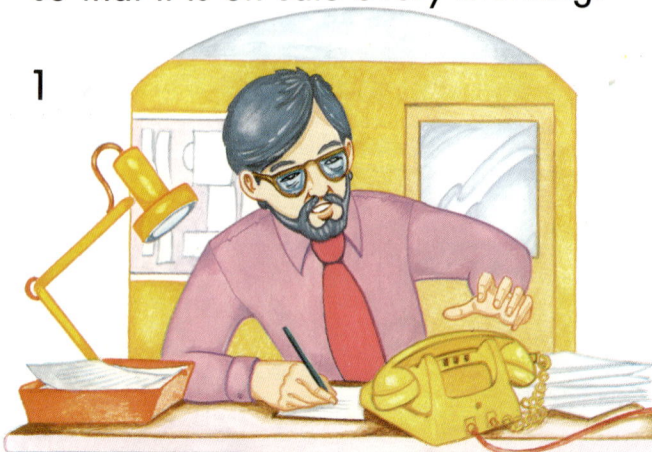

3

The reporter phones the newspaper to tell her story. A typist types it out.

1

People phone up the editor when something interesting is happening.

4

Next, the editor decides how much 'space' to give the story. Important stories take up most of a page.

2

The editor sends a reporter and a photographer to find out more.

5

The stories are keyed into a computer and made into print.

6

The first copies are called 'proofs'. A sub-editor corrects mistakes.

7

The stories are all arranged in the paper. Then the copies are printed.

8

The newspapers are put in vans. They are taken all over the country.

9

The papers arrive early in the morning, and people buy them.

10

Not all newspapers come out every day. Some are Sunday newspapers. Local newspapers report the news for different parts of the country. They are usually printed once a week. People working on these papers do not have to work in such a hurry. Sometimes reporters travel all over the world to report news.

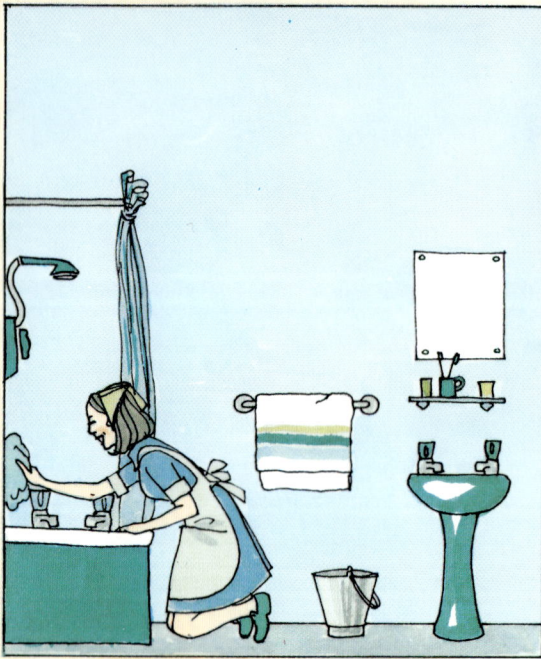

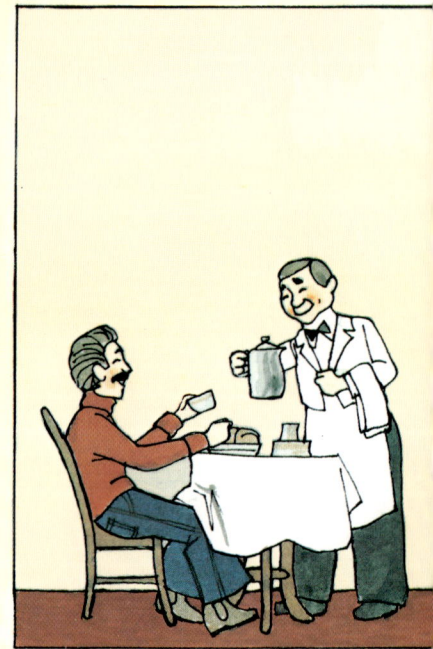

Working in a hotel

When you go to a hotel, the first person you will see is the receptionist. She will see if there is a room for you, and give you the key. Then a porter will carry your suitcase up to your room. Each room has a different door number.

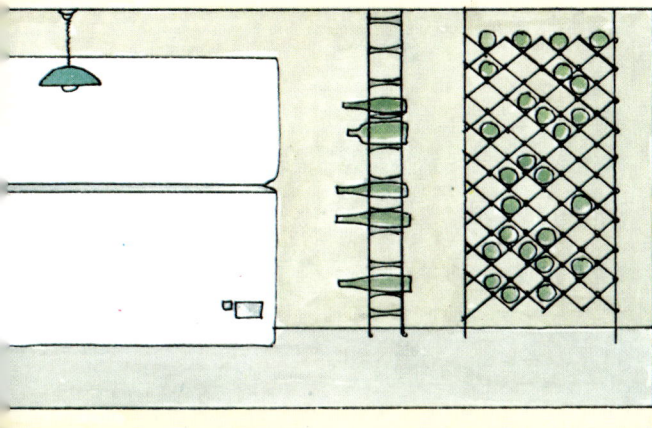

A chambermaid will clean the room and make the bed. In the restaurant, a waiter will show you a menu. This tells you what food the chef is cooking. When you have chosen your meal, he will write down your order and bring it to you. The wine waiter will bring you wine.

DID YOU KNOW?

Not many buildings have their roofs in the clouds. One building in America is 110 storeys high.

The biggest newspaper in the world is the New York Times. The largest copy published weighed 7½ lbs.

A barber's shop in America employs 60 barbers. This is more than in any other barber's shop.

There's a lady in Britain who knits faster than anyone else. One year she made 885 garments.

Super Book is the name of the world's biggest book. It is 9ft high.

INDEX

Ambulance man　52
Animal farming　12, 14
Archaeologist　56-57
Architect　28, 29
Baker　5, 6-7
Bank　58, 59
Barber　8, 64
Bricklayer　28, 31
Butcher　5
Carpenter　28
Cashier　59
Chambermaid　63
Civil engineer　32
Clothes designer　38
Crop farming　12, 16-17
Decorator　29
Department store　10
Doctor　43, 52-53, 54
Dustman　49
Editor　60
Electrician　29
Engineer　32, 33
Factory　6, 34-39
Farmer　12, 16
Fireman　46-47
Fisherman　20, 22-23
Florist　19
Flying doctor　54
Forester　19
Gardener　18

Greengrocer　5
Harvesting　17
Hairdresser　8
Hospital　52-53, 54
Hotel　62
Librarian　43, 51
Lifeboatman　21, 26
Merchant Navy　24
Newspaper　60-61
Nurse　53, 55
Office　34, 40
Oil rig　21, 27
Photographer　60
Physiotherapist　53
Plumber　29, 31
Policeman　42, 44-45
Postman　42, 48
Production line　36
Quantity surveyor　28, 29
Radiographer　53
Receptionist　40, 62
Reporter　60
Restaurant　10, 63
Scientist　56-57
Secretary　41
Shoemaker　9
Supermarket　10
Teacher　43, 50-51
Telephonist　41
Waiter　63
Window dresser　10